First published 2022.

This book is not intended to replace expert medical or legal advice. Expert advice should always be sought in relation to treatment, diagnosis or matters legal in nature.

Part 1

What is menopause?

Chapter 1

Introduction

Menopause and work

Like many women, before I started getting menopause symptoms, I didn't have a good understanding of what to expect from menopause. Until the last couple of years it was considered a taboo subject and a bit embarrassing. Like talking about periods. This was in general, so imagine discussing menopause at work and all of the dynamics that are part of that?! We now have high profile figures like Davina McCall, Mariella Frostrup and Gaby Logan and politicians like Carolyn Harris MP and Caroline Nokes MP in the UK and Amy Schumer and Gayle King in the US talking openly about menopause and raising awareness which is huge progress and helping to open up the conversations.

We all have a part to play in reducing the stigma around menopause in general and also in the workplace, which is a crucial part of making the workplace menopause friendly and retaining capable women in the careers they have worked so hard to build.

I've worked in HR (Human Resources) for thirty years. I've seen far too many women in the menopause transition suffer, and struggle at work (or leave work) because they felt they couldn't cope with their juggling their job, menopause symptoms and possibly family commitments. I've heard too many stories about unsympathetic managers and colleagues, and women being on the receiving end of disparaging and snide comments and stereotypes. It is wearing and over time chips away at what is probably already a fragile confidence for many menopausal women as they make the transition through menopause.

There is a giant lack of information and support in the workplace, with only pockets of good practice. This is not only for the menopausal women themselves, but their managers and colleagues. Menopause is a topic that has been hidden and not talked about for so long, it is not surprising that women don't know what is happening to them, and their managers and colleagues don't know what to say or do. Online resources often focus on medical assistance for menopause, or a superficial adjustment to the work environment, as though putting a fan on a desk or sitting near an open window is the answer to a menopausal woman's workplace challenges.

Mariella Frostrup and Alice Smellie in their fantastic book (a must read) 'Cracking the Menopause: While Keeping Yourself Together, give a fascinating potted history of how society has viewed menopause and menopausal women. It is easy to see why women don't get the support they need and deserve and why menopause has been a taboo subject. We are variously a bit hysterical, mad, witches, and no longer of any use. Sound familiar? We are in a position, particularly in the UK, where there aren't enough people to fill vacant roles. Imagine an entire generation of women being written off because of their age and a manageable condition? As an HR practitioner I have had an insight into how women are viewed at this time in their lives, In discussions about talent and succession, I've had to challenge the notion that because a woman is a certain age, she is likely to be retiring soon and probably not looking for career progression (I should also point out that this happens to women of childbearing age where similarly they can be written off as likely to be out on maternity leave). Some women have babies, and all women go through menopause. We need to get over it.

Our aging workforce and a lack of people to fill roles, makes it even more important to rethink and remove stereotypes about older women. Reading Frostrup and Smellie's book introduced me to a great evolutionary concept called the Grandmother Hypothesis. The hypothesis is based on the view that human women live well past menopause (unlike their closest primate relatives) and can increase their strength and contribution to society. This is because in the times of our ancestors, they were needed to raise and protect their grandchildren while their children hunted for food. Boom. There is a biological and evolutionary basis to our continued value post menopause. I'll take that. Don't misunderstand me, menopause for most women is not fun and is often a challenging transition. Looking back at my experience I'm definitely not going to be telling my girls as they enter menopause 'it was fine, a desk fan and a G&T did the trick'.

I am in the privileged position of being able to influence, and indeed write policy and educate organisations about menopause in the workplace. I hope that you will use whatever influence and voice you have to make the workplace an environment where menopausal women can thrive.

Why this book?

We've still got a long way to go in changing the workplace environment and mindsets to be more positively predisposed to menopausal women, and to be frank about it, I've written this book because I'm angry. I'm angry because it's the 21st Century and we still aren't talking about menopause openly at work, and in some places, suggesting that it's inappropriate to discuss it. As an HR practitioner, I'm still advising against performance management conversations involving women who are clearly suffering from menopause symptoms and hearing about flexible working requests being declined when they would do so much to retain talented and capable women in the workplace. I could talk about the unfairness of this treatment and the potential for discrimination and legal interventions. I could draw your attention to the morality of saying to a large portion of the workforce (50% in fact) that we've finished with you now thank you very much. If you can't conform to a workplace designed around a workforce in their 20 something peak physical condition, you're no longer fit for purpose. If this isn't enough to sway you towards a belief that understanding and supporting menopause in the workplace is the right thing to do, there is a growing economic imperative that might tip the balance for you. The younger generations joining the workforce are themselves demanding a different way of working. They want flexibility and work life balance.

Suddenly there is a critical mass of workers demanding change, and as employers we need to listen. There are more jobs than there are workers to fill them. Unless we prioritise inclusion in the workplace, organisations will grind to a halt where there are not enough people to fill roles as older workers decide that they have had enough and leave work, taking experience, knowledge, and capacity with them.

The new world of work

Since the pandemic, the younger generations in the workplace have made their voice loud and clear. A traditional 9 to 5, five days a week working model is not what they want, and they know this is not how they produce their best work. Older generations pour scorn on this with accusations of laziness and lack of commitment, but the research on hybrid and flexible working does not support this view. It may be a perceived loss of control for employers and a fear of change that drive the naysayers to stick to the traditional model of fixed working patterns, but that doesn't mean we shouldn't change.

Any successful change management involves education and empathy. My aim for this book is that I can educate on the impact that menopause has on women in the workplace and the reasons we should change, through the tribe of generous people who contributed directly, or indirectly to the information within. It provides information on what happens to women during the menopause, and the possible impact in the workplace. I've deliberately steered away from information and advice on medical support such as HRT. I'm not a clinician and there are books and resources that will provide that guidance. At the back of the book there are links to resources and clinicians who can advise you. This work is specifically about managing menopause in the workplace and is aimed at women experiencing menopause at work, their colleagues, managers and decision makers and budget holders who can provide resources.

While we are on the subject of the new world of work, I have referred to women in the context of experiencing menopause throughout this book, but I recognise that there will be many people who experience menopause who do not identify as women. This book is for you also.

My story

My own story is another driver behind this book, and I will share my experiences with you throughout. My life has changed so much over the past few years. Not long ago I was desperate to stop working I was so exhausted and stressed. After years of health problems combined with menopause, I felt I had nothing left in my energy bank. Now at almost 55 I am doing work that I am most proud of in my career and I am thriving. I don't want to give the impression that I feel fantastic every day, that isn't the case. With the help of colleagues and menopause practitioners like Aly Dilks at Simply Menopausal, I have developed strategies for coping with my menopause and reframed the way I look at my life and work. I am more confident in asking for what I need to thrive, and I know how to ask for it. The job I do means that I have more control over my work pattern and environment although I appreciate that women in other sectors and roles may not have this luxury. I hope that there are some elements of this book that you will find helpful, and that the owners of businesses and line managers will read this book and learn what they can do to make conditions better.

In my younger years I had endometriosis, polycystic ovaries and other gynecological conditions, all conditions that many women battle through during their working lives. In my forties, I had hypothyroidism and hyperparathyroidism which had similar symptoms to menopause so it is difficult for me to say for sure when my peri-menopause began. I feel like I have been a slave to my hormones for most of my adult (working) life. Add into the mix miscarriage and infertility treatment, I don't feel like I have had many periods of my adult life where my hormones have been balanced and stable. Things are starting to change (albeit slowly) with campaigning and education provided by tv programmes like the ones recently made by Davina McCall and Mariella Frostrup, which have helped to highlight that having an imbalance in hormones is likely to be debilitating and needs to the appropriate treatment. As Menopause Nurse Specialist Aly Dilks said to me, I have a lifelong underactive thyroid because my thyroid is deficient in thyroxine. I wouldn't expect to function without the levothyroxine I take to replace the deficiency, so why would I try to function without replacing the other hormones that I am deficient in such as oestrogen? It's a good point, yet I struggled to get a diagnosis for menopause, and even after I got the diagnosis, it was a couple of years before I was prescribed HRT. I am very clear of my menopause (the end of my periods) however, as that was surgical. At 51 after years of debilitating gynae problems I had a full hysterectomy and nothing prepared me for that.

A surgical menopause strips out your remaining hormone balance virtually overnight, without the steadier transition of a biological menopause. To add to my (quite literal) pain, following the surgery, the gynecologist told me that I wasn't able to go back onto HRT straight away, to allow the endometriosis to die back, although I've be advised since, that it was possible to have HRT and that on balance it would have been much better to do that. In addition to the endometriosis, I had adenomyosis, fibroids and my right ovary was stuck to the back of my womb. While it was a huge relief to end the pain and infertility that had blighted my adult life, my hormones were all over the place.

My calcium levels were slightly raised which was the signpost that I had a parathyroid tumour which was also causing huge disruption to my body including gallstones, problems with my bones and hormone imbalance. By the time I was 54, I had had a severe GI bleed, gall bladder removed, full hysterectomy and a discectomy in my lumbar spine which has left me with very little sensation in my left leg. I'm sharing this not because I'm wearing it as a badge of honour, but because my story is very common to women of around my age. Things start breaking and stop working, and in our 40s and 50s our bodies are changing. We often develop other conditions that add to the symptoms of menopause. We may have caring responsibilities and are trying to manage our work lives and that is incredibly tough alongside other health problems that manifest themselves at this stage of life. Women are less likely to seek medical advice and often try and battle on until they are really unwell. If you are a woman struggling with work and some of these conditions, or a colleague or employer of a woman in this situation, give yourself and them, credit for having managed to keep going under exceptionally difficult circumstances. You/they are awesome. But being awesome doesn't mean that you should have to struggle without support. There are solutions to many of these challenges and the theme of this book is that women can thrive at work during menopause with the right information and support from colleagues, the organisation, and their families.

Why this book?

This book is a combination of information and insights, working on the basis that with knowledge comes understanding and possible solutions can be achieved.

The information and insights are included throughout the book, but I have set the context and provided a case for change in the first two chapters, **Introduction** and **What is**

menopause and how is it impacting the workplace. As well as developing an understanding of menopause symptoms and impact, it will provide information that could be used to support a business case for funding for a menopause programme, or justification for a menopause policy and manager guide. The remainder of the book is structured into 10 steps that will help organisations to put in place a comprehensive menopause programme and the justification for doing so. I have used recognised change management techniques and models throughout to help the implementation of the programme and to make it stick, and models of organisation culture to show how initiatives become embedded in organisations and become the way things are done.

I've already shared that I decided to write this book because of my frustration that so many people in the workplace know so little about menopause and how to provide support in the workplace. But for frustration, don't read judgement. This book is written from a place of support, understanding and recognition that women should not be written off, nor write themselves off during the menopause transition. There may be women who have not been able to secure the help they need to continue in the workplace and who choose to opt out. I wish you all the best and sincerely hope that your decision was a choice and that you were not forced out by a lack of support and understanding, or worse still, that you were managed out. Much of the research I will draw on in this book and the stories I will share do not describe a workplace where compassion and understanding are front and centre. The reasons for this aren't clear and may well be an area for future research. I hope that the gap between workplace practice and the needs of menopausal women are caused by a lack of understanding and knowledge, rather than a shortsighted focus on working in an outdated model of work that employers cling to at their peril.

Chapter 2
What is menopause and how is it impacting the workplace?

My experience of the workplace

My work has always relied very heavily on my ability to think, solve problems, stay calm under pressure and focus. These are all attributes that quite often get lost during the menopause transition. We visualize ourselves in a particular way at home and at work, and when we age, our perception of ourselves changes. My body is a different shape; I'm 3 stone heavier than I was in the early part of my career. I need time to process information, that pre-menopause I could have processed in minutes and unless it's minus 10 outside, my ability to wear knitwear is long gone. They may seem trivial and superficial worries (which of course they are) but they have changed how I see myself at work. The potential to forget words or names of people and feeling confident are rightly or wrongly, very important parts of our work persona. Much of our self-esteem and feelings of belonging are wrapped up in our work, so when that changes, it can have a huge impact on our wellbeing.

I had felt the decline in my health and abilities very slowly and very subtly since I was about 46. I could burst into tears at the drop of a hat and the exhaustion was overwhelming. Insomnia and overthinking during the night and feeling dysfunctional and like a zombie during the day. The parathyroid tumour I had but didn't know I had exacerbated my symptoms. When I look back over the 6 years between 2014 and 2020 I don't know how I managed to achieve all the things that I did.

I can look back on that phase now and see the positives of managing to achieve things with overwhelming physical challenges, but until recently, and especially during that time, I felt immense shame. My memory was poor, I was ridiculously emotional, I couldn't concentrate and numerous other symptoms on top of my exhaustion meant that I couldn't do my job in the way that I had done for most of my career. I felt a failure and that made me feel ashamed and that I had let everyone down, especially myself. If I could advise my younger early menopausal self and you the readers about how to manage this situation differently, there are a few key points:

This is normal - you are normal. Not everyone will get the same symptoms or in the same way, but the body is changing and the fluctuation in hormones is causing disruption.
Understand the new normal - educating myself on symptoms and the impact of those symptoms was a great starting point in helping to frame the circumstances and adapt to how things are and how things will be in the future.
Get evidence about what is happening - a blood test is a great starting point. While it's not suitable as a diagnosis of menopause, it

helped to provide a picture of how my body was functioning. In my case there were other things going on. I had an undiagnosed underactive thyroid, a parathyroid tumour and I was anemic. All of this was causing a perfect storm in my body alongside the endometriosis and polycystic ovaries, all of which cause hormonal imbalance and needed managing.
Talk - talk to people who can help you understand what is happening, and how to manage things. Like many women I thought I was suffering either with a mental health condition or early dementia. I thought I was too young for menopause. No one told me that it is a transition that happens over years. In fact, people don't talk about it at all, which perpetuates myths and misunderstandings and helps to keep what is a normal stage of life, taboo.

What is menopause?

Menopause is described by the NHS in the UK as the point where periods stop because of lower hormone levels. This usually happens between the ages of 45-55, but it is important to remember that we are all different and it is possible to experience menopause symptoms outside this age range. Terminology about menopause can be confusing and I have heard many stories from women who have been told they are not menopausal even though their bodies are producing the most debilitating symptoms. Often this is a misunderstanding of terminology, particularly what is menopause and what is perimenopause.

Menopause: the point where a woman is no longer getting her periods, usually for 12 months or more.
Perimenopause: the phase up to when periods have stopped for 12 months or more.

In the US, the Office on Women's Health describe the reason for this transition as the body producing less oestrogen and progesterone. The reduction of both hormones can cause debilitating symptoms. In the case of a surgical menopause, there is no gradual buildup of symptoms over time, and women are plunged straight into menopause. A surgical menopause is caused by the woman having a full hysterectomy where the ovaries are removed. It is the ovaries that produce oestrogen and progesterone hence their removal triggers menopause. Some cancer treatments can also trigger menopause such as chemotherapy. Over the last few years, menopause has begun to be described more helpfully as menopause transition which more accurately describes menopause as a period of change.

Menopause symptoms

Menopause symptoms can be different for different women and can come with varying levels of severity. The following is not an exhaustive list, but most women will experience a number of these symptoms (if not all) during their menopause transition:

1. Changes to your periods

The first sign of the perimenopause is usually, but not always, a change in the normal pattern of your periods, for example they may become irregular, heavier or lighter. You might get periods several weeks apart or several months apart making it difficult to track a normal cycle. Eventually you'll stop having periods altogether, at when this has been for a period of 12 months or more, this is what's known as the menopause.

2. Mental health symptoms

Many women report feeling very down and not able to function to the level they had been previously. Many women I have talked to about menopause say that they feel as though they have dementia which can be incredibly worrying and difficult to manage in the workplace.

Common mental health symptoms of menopause and perimenopause include:

- changes to your mood, for example, low mood, anxiety, mood swings and low self-esteem
- problems with memory or concentration (brain fog) and difficulty with finding the right words for things

3. Physical symptoms

Common physical symptoms of menopause and perimenopause include:

- hot flushes or flashes in the US, when you have sudden feelings of hot or cold in your face, neck and chest which can make you dizzy
- difficulty sleeping, which may be a result of night sweats and make you feel tired and irritable during the day
- palpitations, when your heartbeats suddenly become more noticeable

- headaches and migraines that are worse than usual
- muscle aches and joint pains
- changing body shape and weight gain
- skin changes including dry and itchy skin
- reduced sex drive
- vaginal dryness and pain, itching or discomfort during sex
- recurrent urinary tract infections (UTIs)

Reproduced from the NHS Menopause symptoms
https://www.nhs.uk/conditions/menopause/symptoms/

Symptoms in the workplace

It is shocking the number of people (women included) who are not familiar with what the menopause transition is and how it affects us. Menopause has been such a taboo subject in the past that it's not surprising. But it's also not helpful for effective management if we don't know what is happening to us and why, as well as being able to receive support from managers in the workplace. Menopause transition must be discussed honestly and openly in the workplace. If we don't, we continue to risk negative impacts on both women and the workplace. The size of the problem facing women and employers shouldn't be underestimated. A report published by the UK Government Women and Equalities Committee in July 2022 highlighted that if women leave the workplace during menopause, not only is there a loss of knowledge and skills, but there is an impact on the gender pay gap, pensions gap and the number of women in leadership. The report quotes research carried out by health care provider BUPA which found that 900,000 women had left work because of their menopause symptoms. That is a huge section of the workforce, with knowledge and skills that would take years to replace, even if there were available candidates.

Top 10 symptoms

It doesn't take a stretch of the imagination to see how these symptoms could disrupt a woman's ability to thrive in the workplace, whether it's cognitive challenges or physical. As I write, we are in the middle of a heatwave which combined with my hot flushes is making writing slow going while I try to cool down, writing in early morning and later in the evening, and moving around the house and garden to avoid the sun.

A study carried out in the UK by researchers at Nottingham University investigated the experience of women transitioning through the menopause in the workplace. The study found that of a list of 19 menopause symptoms, the top 10 of the most disruptive symptoms amongst the respondents were:

1. Poor concentration	50.9%
2. Tiredness	50.7%
3. Poor memory	50.5%
4. Feeling low/depressed	41.9%
5. Lowered confidence	38.9%
6. Sleep disturbances	37.3%
7. Irritability	35.6%
8. Hot flushes	35.1%
9. Joint and muscular aches	31.3%
10. Mood swings	29.0%

It is very helpful to see these symptoms listed in order of disruption to the women surveyed. The common perception of women suffering menopause symptoms at work, are having a hot flush which can be resolved with a desk fan. Now don't misunderstand me, I fully appreciate the pain of an unexpected flush making an untimely appearance and have a great deal of respect for those women having flushes in full PPE (personal protection equipment) or chefing in a stifling hot kitchen, but it is the tip of the iceberg from a work perspective. Hot flushes are less likely to cause you problems when it comes to your performance or applying for a promotion. Cognitive symptoms such as poor concentration and memory compounded by tiredness are clearly a much concerning problem to the women surveyed and many of the women I talk to, and they warrant more discussion and attention than desk fans.

These are all incredibly unhelpful symptoms to have while you are trying to carry out your job and possibly run a home, but there are interventions and adjustments that can be put into place relatively easily to make working life more enjoyable and manageable. We will talk about these and management of other symptoms throughout this book. So, what is the size of the problem we are talking about and why should we care?

How does this impact the workplace?

According to a study by Koru Kids, 18% of the women surveyed were trying to find a way to leave their jobs reported People Management Magazine (1). The researchers estimated that there are at least 5.87 million women of peri or menopause age working in the UK. In a payrolled workforce of 29.6 million that is a sizable chunk. Not only are those employees looking for a way out, but they are also continuing to struggle at work with their symptoms.

I hope that you will be influenced by the moral duty to create a workplace where everyone can thrive. We are talking about a transition that will affect at least 50% of the population at some point and to some degree. It could be you, your partner, colleague, mum, sister, friend. This is not a rare or exclusive health condition; it's likely to have affected someone you know if not yourself and I am sure that many people will read this book with the intention of creating the right environment because it's the right thing to do. Here are some other reasons for supporting women in the workplace during the menopause transition:

1. The Great Resignation

If you need a little more persuasion, and some economic evidence, consider the current work situation and google 'The Great Resignation'. Following the end of the pandemic, many surveys carried out by major research organisations cite the number of employees intending to look for alternative work. Job seekers are more discerning in their requirements from a role. They want flexibility, creative and motivating workplaces and to work for organisations and work that have purpose.

2. The Labour Market

The combination of the impact on the labour market of Brexit in the UK and the pandemic worldwide, has led to there being more job vacancies that there are people to do them. As of May 2022, there are more vacancies and less people available for work (i.e., looking and fit for work). Of course, it does not correspond that those people available for work have the right skills and experience for the vacancies, but in short, there are more vacancies than people to fill them. Why would organisations not do everything they could to nurture their precious talent? It is a job seeker's market. This delta between roles and people won't change if we head into a recession.

3. Talent and a recession

It is a myth that during a recession there is a greater availability of talent. Research shows that good people stay put during a recession or they leave the workforce altogether. The group of employees we are talking about in this book are most likely to either leave the workforce altogether or do something completely different. That is a big loss of skills and experience from the workforce and equally, economic activity. If even a small percentage of the 5.9 million economically active women leave the workforce in the UK, this will have a huge impact on the economy because of the impact on job vacancies not filled and buying power.

4. Menopause and the economy

I'm hoping that most people who read this book will be supportive of doing their best for menopausal women in the workplace purely because it's the right thing to do, but I am also aware that often there is a dichotomy between doing the right thing for the individual and the right thing for the organisation. It is my view that there compelling reasons that benefit both and that they are inextricably linked.

I've touched on the Great Resignation, and at the time of writing, there are more vacant roles that there are people to fill them. Given the restrictions on workforce migration, this isn't likely to change soon. Add into the mix that many countries have an ageing workforce, it doesn't take a statistician to work out that a large section of the available workforce pool is likely to be women of menopausal age. This is supported by a UK Government report into the economic impact of menopause 'Menopause at Work', which shows that there is an increase in women in employment in mid-life. If these women choose to leave the workforce, we will have an even great deficit of workers than currently, if they stay and suffer with their symptoms, engagement and productivity will inevitably suffer.

The impact on the economy is both to individuals and to organisations and the wider country economy. Women leave or lose their jobs because of symptoms or stay in their jobs trying to cope with their symptoms which could affect productivity, or their ability to seek promotion, affecting both earning power and the number of women available for leadership positions. The 30% Club provides great research and insights into how much more effectively organisations with women on the board operate. In summary, women are important to retain in the workplace, and in order to retain them during the menopause transition, organisations need to have a programme of support in place.

In the next sections, I will take you through how to set up a menopause programme and how to manage menopause in the workplace.

Part 2

Designing a Menopause Programme

Chapter 3

Developing a menopause stakeholder plan

One of the big things I've learned from talking to women about menopause, and the research and reading I've done, is that menopause is a different experience for everyone. While there are lists of symptoms that are commonly experienced by many women, how those symptoms are experienced is different from woman to woman. Developing an off the shelf programme may not lead to the changes you want with the same impact. if you want to develop a meaningful programme that is embedded in your organisation's culture, your starting point is to speak to and gather the views and input of the people that have a stake in it. In other words, a 'stakeholder'.

What is a stakeholder?

My go to book for change management is **'The Effective Change Manager's Handbook'** edited by Richard Smith and others. The definition of a stakeholder given in the book is that a stakeholder is a person or group of people with an interest in the change you are working on. In this case that is obviously those employees experiencing menopause, but this is not the total story. Other individual employees and groups of employees also have an interest in the development and outcomes of a menopause programme. In general people are much more engaged with a change if they have been involved with and have collaborated on its development. While introducing a menopause programme isn't necessarily controversial, anything new is still a change, and people, quite rightly, often want to have some input. Missing individuals or groups out, could lead to problems further down the line or the potential for sabotage.

You may work in a small or medium sized business where it seems clearer who the stakeholders are or a global corporate where there is a complex network of groups and structures, but either way, spending time deciding who those key stakeholders are, and what level of involvement they need is vital preparation in bringing the right people round the table.
There are four parts to creating a plan for managing stakeholders:

1. **Brainstorm** - the purpose is to create a long list of possible stakeholders that may need to have some involvement in the development of menopause programme.
2. **Segment** - at this stage, you will begin to put your long list of stakeholders into a group based on their level of involvement in the programme.
3. **Prioritise -** when you have segmented your stakeholders into groups, you then need to prioritise them by factors such as frequency of

contact and level of power to influence the programme.

4. Engagement plan - having a plan enables you to ensure that tasks and meetings happen by particular dates and are running alongside the development of your menopause programme.

Brainstorming: Identifying who your stakeholders are

You are at the beginning point of developing your programme, and it's likely that you have a few people you will be either working with or gaining input from. Since the pandemic we quite often work away from what was our normal office environment and are more inclined to gather information remotely by email. It is one approach, identifying stakeholders needs discussion. There are lots of questions to ask when identifying groups of stakeholders. Are there any individuals in the groups that may be able to add expertise, or support, or on the other hand, cause problems. Doing all of this by email would be a huge task and could lead to extremely lengthy email trails. it would be more effective and efficient to facilitate a group session either online by MS Teams or Zoom, or another similar platform, or face to face. I love a whiteboard and post it notes, which used to be the downside of online workshops, but many platforms now have integrated whiteboards and there are online post it note platforms (many of which are free) such as Miro.

My favourite method for brainstorming ideas is mind mapping. Miro has an online mind map and with a mind map, the branches of the map can be used to put the stakeholders into segments that you will then decide how, when, and how much you communicate with, and involve in the programme. Keep in mind that this list is likely to change over time. For example, if you are involving a Benefits and

Reward Team in a menopause programme, they may have more involvement up front as discussions happen about the possibility of procuring a healthcare or wellbeing provider for example, which then declines as the provision becomes live.

Segmenting: Dividing your stakeholders into groups

As a starting point, I've suggested a list of possible stakeholders in a menopause programme, but you should not take this for granted. Use the template I have provided as a template and a list of possible stakeholders as a starting point for your discussions. Organisations are different and this is an important exercise in managing the groups of people that could be affected or involved in the programme. Below is the list I created of possible stakeholders in a menopause programme:

1. Menopausal women
2. Human Resources. HR is a broad range of disciplines under the banner, so I have expanded HR into a list of possible parts within the function that might be involved - HR Business Partnering, HR Operations, Policy Makers, Compensation and Benefits/Reward, Learning and Development.
3. Occupational Health.
4. Line Managers.
5. Finance.
6. Colleagues.
7. Trades unions.

As you can see this is a broad group of people and they will need to be managed differently. For example, some of the group will have a direct interest in a menopause programme, some will need to approve decisions, some will just want to know what is happening but at a high level. When you have a list, put the names of the people you have identified into categories which will determine how often you will engage with them, and at what level. This is known as 'Stakeholder Mapping'.

Prioritising: Creating a communication plan by mapping your stakeholders

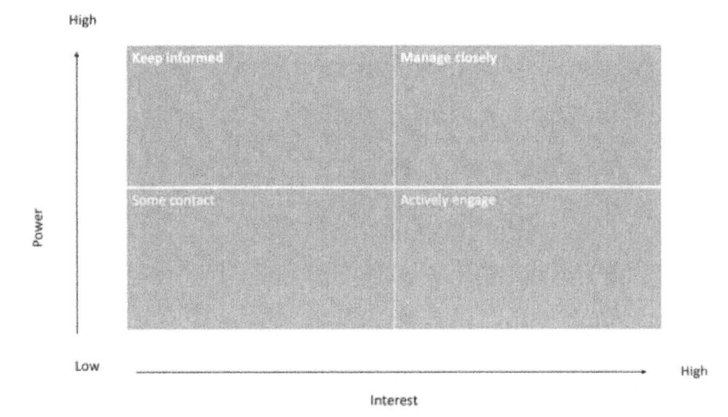

Stakeholder mapping is all about prioritising your engagement with your stakeholders by:

1. **Interest** - how much interest do they have in the development of a menopause programme? Will they have direct involvement or is it more a

case of needing to know that it's happening, but not the detail.

2. **Power** - how much power do they have? Power is not just about the hierarchical position a person holds in an organisation. Power could mean that an individual or group of individuals have influence and the ability to speed up or slow down a project.

Put the names of the individuals or group onto post it notes. If an individual or group has high power and high interest, for example when developing a menopause programme, this could be a women's and LGBTQ+ affinity group, place the post it note into 'manage closely.' This is a group that has a direct interest and will need close involvement from start to finish.

If there are individuals or groups where the information and involvement is less, put the post it notes into the 'some contact' box. For example, line managers. You may want to let them know that the programme is happening, and you may want their view on what resources they would find helpful when managing colleagues during the menopause transition, but they may not be directly involved throughout the programme. Of course, I am using these groups as examples and when you do your own stakeholder mapping, it is subjective and based on the circumstances of your own organisation and the groups and individuals involved. Next you need to create a plan.

Engagement: Creating a plan

An engagement plan gives an overview of who will engage with who, which helps to prevent individuals or groups missing out on inputting into what is a very important programme. Having a box that shows the status (red, amber, green) of the engagement also helps the project teams to make sure that it is on track.

Stakeholder	Status	Area of influence/ interest	Project stage	Responsible	Approach	Method	Frequency
Menopausal people	On track	Will changes benefit the group? What are their needs?	Ongoing	Project lead	Consult and inform	Focus groups, email updates, meetings	Frequent
Compensation & benefits	At risk	Own the policy and provide resources through benefits programme	Planning (and sign off)	Project team member	Consult and inform	Workshop, email updates	Regular
Occupational Health	Caution	Advise on management of symptoms in the workplace	Planning (and sign off)	Project lead	Consult and inform	Workshop, email updates	Less frequent
Line Managers	Caution	Will use guidance and provide support	Planning	Project team member	Consult	Focus groups, email updates	Occasional
Finance	Caution	Will sign off budget for any resources needed	Planning (and sign off)	Project lead	Consult, inform, approve costs	Meetings and email updates	Occasional
Colleagues	Caution	Will support menopausal colleagues	Planning	Project team member	Inform	Email updates	Occasional
Trade unions/employee council	On track	Will advise on content and support menopausal colleagues	Planning and sign off	Project lead/HR	Consult and inform	Workshop, email updates and meetings	Frequent
Employee Resource Groups	On track	Will advise on content and support menopausal colleagues	Planning and sign off	Project lead/HR	Consult and inform	Workshops, email and meetings	Frequent

Example of a stakeholder engagement plan for the development of a menopause programme

Using the information you gained about who your stakeholders are and how and when you need to communicate with them, you can add this to your plan.

Getting people on board with a menopause programme is vital to achieving the aim of creating an environment where menopausal women can thrive. Policies, guides, and other tools are all meaningless if people aren't on board. Different groups and individuals will have different views and needs for involvement, which is why engaging with them at an early stage and throughout is so critical.

Use your plan to keep your stakeholders engaged throughout the process, but make sure it's a dynamic document. Review it often and make amendments as necessary. Organisations and people change, and as you work through the programme you may want to add people and actions. If you get this part right, you will create and engage a group of people who will support the outcomes of your programme and become champions for menopause in the workplace.

Summary

- At the beginning of your programme, brainstorm a list of stakeholders and prioritise the level of engagement with them based on how and when, and what the engagement will look like.

- Divide your stakeholders into groups, and tailor your engagement plan around the needs of the group. For example, your engagement and discussions with menopausal women to gather information and views, are likely to be different from the ones you have with line managers.
- Your plan will show how you will prioritise the engagement with your stakeholders by importance and their level of power.
- Now you are ready to develop an engagement plan that shows:
- How you will engage
- Who you will engage with
- Who will do the engagement
- How frequently the engagement will happen

Chapter 4
Developing a vision for menopause at work

I previously mentioned that menopause has been a taboo subject and has only recently been talked about openly in the media. Discussion about menopause in the workplace is changing and with the implementation of a high-profile menopause policy by Channel 4 in 2019, many other organisations have followed. However, menopause is still a subject that is not widely known about and rarely discussed in many workplaces work. Given the perceived sensitivity of the subject, and the lack of knowledge, asking managers and colleagues to talk openly about menopause is probably a step to far without a programme of education and change. This must be more than another policy that sits on a portal. To effect real change and create an environment where menopausal women can thrive, organisations must bring their approach to menopause to life with a comprehensive programme; a programme that is driven by supportive leadership with visible menopause role models.

What is a vision and why is it important?

A vision shows the organisation what the workplace will look like in the future state. A story that helps employees understand where the organisation is heading and what will happen to get it there. Often when change happens, or is needed, it's only discussed in meeting rooms behind closed door, with select groups of people. We all see things so differently it can be challenging to mobilise a whole organisation in the same direction at the same time. Parts of your employee population won't know what it feels like to be menopausal and because of the stigma around discussing women's health, may have very limited information about menopause, or only ever have been exposed to the myths. If you write a policy and do nothing else, it's easy to see how nothing will change. It's as inaccessible as Narnia to a significant number of people. To make a noticeable difference to the workplace for menopausal women, everyone needs to understand the journey the organisation is on, how you will get there and what it will look and feel like when you do.

Developing the vision

The first step in creating a vision, is to develop an understanding of why things need to change. How does it feel to be a menopausal woman in your workplace? What are the challenges and the barriers to thriving? The best way of understanding all of this is to ask. This might be through focus groups perhaps, or a questionnaire depending on the size of your organisation. Getting direct feedback is the perfect way of involving a critical group of stakeholders and making sure that you are creating a message that will resonate with them (because you've crafted it around their feedback).

Your vision will set out what the organisation will look and feel like after you have changed, what people will do and how the change will happen. For example, in the context of our menopause programme, some of the points you might want to cover are:

1. You've asked menopausal women what it feels like at the organisation now, and what they would like it to feel like with the changes in place. Your messaging will be more authentic if you have sought and included feedback from the group menopause affects the most.

2. Perhaps the group has told you in the feedback that they would like some adjustments to how they work to make

it easier to perform at their best. As a result of this, in the new world, flexible/hybrid working will be automatic so that women can work according to the best time of the day for them.

3. Part of the feedback you have received might have been that managers feel uncomfortable in talking to their menopausal employees so either the conversations don't happen, or they are not good quality conversations. One of the outcomes of the change that you will want to talk about in your vision, is that all managers will receive training on menopause, and managing conversations about menopause.

Your vision statement is a call to action. It should mobilise the organisation to make a commitment to support the changes you are proposing. In summary, your vision should include:

- An overview of the problem.
- What will be different after the change.
- What process you will follow to make the change and who will be involved.

Example vision statement for a retail organisation

> **Every woman will experience menopause. As a major retailer with a store in every town many of those women work for us. Over 70% of our workforce are women, and 30% of that population are at the age they are likely to be going through the menopause transition. We recognise the importance of our workforce and making sure that we help them to stay well and to feel included,**

whatever the stage of their lives. We listened to feedback from our employees currently in menopause and we realised we need to do more to help them to feel supported and to thrive. We know that menopause is a subject that hasn't been talked about widely and has often been stigmatised, and the feedback told us that just writing a policy wouldn't be enough to make a real difference.

Using this feedback and expert advice we will develop a menopause programme that will ensure that our managers and colleagues are educated on menopause, how it affects women in the workplace and how they can support, and have good quality, open and meaningful conversations. The programme will make sure that we source and secure an occupational health provider that understands how menopause symptoms can be managed in our working environment and communicate this in a clear and accessible way to both our employees and our line managers. The roles that many of our employees do is physically demanding and our stores are open for long hours. We will look at our uniforms and the impact they have on menopausal women, the working environment and rest areas to help our menopausal employees manage the impact of their symptoms at work more effectively.

We have gathered a project group who will work on developing the elements of the programme which will be created around the feedback we have received from our menopausal employees and their colleagues and managers, along with experts in the field of menopause. The programme will be developed over the next two months, and we expect to launch in October in time for World Menopause Day when we will have a series of events to celebrate the launch of the programme. We have set up a dedicated email address to answer your questions and listen to any suggestions you have, and an area on our employee portal to keep you updated on what is happening.

This is an exciting and valuable step in our journey to becoming a menopause friendly employer, and another stage in our commitment to listening to your needs and creating an organisation we are all proud to work for.

A vision statement is likely to need to be applicable to different audiences, some of whom may not have any experience of the change, in this case menopause or the facilities that are being proposed in your programme. Bringing the vision to life, means that more of your employee's groups will commit to the changes you are proposing and participate.

Bringing the vision to life

Most organisations will have different audiences within them, and your message will need to be accessible to all of those groups. For example, if you work in a global organisation, the language you use in one country, may not be appropriate in another. There are different terms for menopause and menopause symptoms in different cultures, and in some countries, there is no word for menopause. Consider the language you use carefully and ask your key stakeholders how to get the message across in the most effective way.

Keep the language simple and avoid terms such as medical terms, that your audience may not understand. Your vision statement shouldn't be excessively long (around one A4 page) if you want to keep the attention of the audience, but you might feel that it would help gaining commitment to the changes by, for example, providing some more detailed information about the menopause and how it affects women in the workplace. You could do this be developing a separate tool such as a video or online presentation that provides more detailed information and allows you to keep your vision statement succinct.

Many organisations use 'personas' to help them tell the story of what things will look like in the future. A persona is a fictional character that is used to illustrate a particular situation.

You describe who they are, give them a name, and a photograph from stock images. You might describe their role, where they work and the challenges that they are experiencing. You develop the story using your persona to illustrate how things will be different in the new world.

Example persona for a menopause programme

Sarah

Sarah is 48 and works as a manager of a retail store where she spends a great deal of her time managing a team, moving stock around and serving customers. She has worked in retail her whole career and is highly experienced and knowledgeable.

Sarah's frustrations:

Sarah is often exhausted as she works long 12 hour shifts to make sure she is always available for questions from her team and since her perimenopause started, she has been suffering with back pain in her lower back. During the summer, her ankles were swollen because she was spending so much time on her feet, and she struggles to remember the names of the products as her memory has been affected by menopause. Her Area Manager seemed to be embarrassed the time that Sarah mentioned her menopause, so she hasn't raised it again and struggles on.

What Sarah needs:

- Her manager to be trained in having a positive conversation confidently about menopause.
- Support to manage her physical symptoms via an occupational health professional.
- A conversation with her manager to discuss possible adjustments in her hours and working practices.

- A risk assessment and the involvement of health and safety to look at how her working environment can be adjusted to support her physical symptoms.

Our menopause programme will provide:

- Line manager training on menopause.
- Occupational health assessments.
- Menopause friendly policies, guidance and resources.
- Menopause specific risk assessments.

Having personas is a way of making a change appear three dimensional to your employees as long as long as you make them realistic.

If the programme you are proposing needs resources that requires funding and incur other indirect costs such has hours to implement, you may need to develop a business case to secure money from your leadership team or budget holders. This is the stage of your project where should be thinking about a business case.

Building a business case

A business case is the justification for providing funds for a project, or sometimes, it may not involve funds but could be the justification for a project going ahead and involvement of your stakeholders. It is likely to cover the benefits to the business, any potential costs, risks to the project, different options and the reasoning particular options are being recommended.

It is likely to include the following elements:

1. The business context - what is the reason for the change and how will the change impact the business. For a menopause programme, you might include some information about how menopause is affecting the business. This could be that you have a gender pay gap because high numbers of women are leaving the business and are losing talented and capable women from your workforce. You are finding it difficult to attract women leaders to the business.

2. **Return on investment** - how will the business gain a return on the investment it makes in the proposed project? You may focus on a reduction of recruitment and training costs by retaining employees and reducing sick days.
3. **Finance and cost** - what will the project cost to manage, and the potential cost options, with a justification for the option chosen.
4. **Implementation** - how will the project be managed and implemented? What are the timescales and how will governance be managed? How many hours are needed to work on the project and deliver it?

A business case is the why, the what, the who and the how of your project. Once you have developed your business case and it is signed off by the decision makers in your business, and created and communicated your vision, you are ready to go.

Part 3

Managing Menopause at Work

Chapter 5
Understanding menopause symptoms in a work context

Thankfully it's becoming easier to find information about menopause and managing symptoms, although there is still much more to do to make it a mainstream and accessible topic. When I started to search for information about managing symptoms in a work context, I found that the discussions tended to focus on flushes, with many references made to desk fans and room temperature as solutions. I recently listened to the experience of UK politicians Ian Duncan Smith MP and Wes Streeting MP wearing a menopause vest (known as a MenoVest) for an event organised by Carolyn Harris MP. The MenoVest is designed to imitate the impact of hot flushes, and after seeing it in action, it's clear that hot flushes are a symptom that can more easily replicated if you want your audience to feel and experience one of the symptoms of menopause. Hot flushes are probably the most widely known symptom and not a pleasant experience at any time, and especially in the workplace, but referring to the research I cited in the previous chapter, top of the list of disruptive symptoms at work is poor concentration.

How menopause symptoms affect work

Concentration is something I found increasingly difficult in the early part of my menopause transition. Like many women, I was juggling lots of balls with family and work, and multi-tasking is expected as a normal part of our day to day lives. I know I'm not the only woman who forgot to pick up a child from school or forgot about a meeting or appointment I was due at. I'm sure that multi-tasking effectively is a myth, but it becomes much more of a challenge during menopause. My cognitive ability has always been a crucial part of my work as an HR Director, and if this falls below what is necessary to perform, or worse still, fails, it's a major problem. I have good days and I have bad days which I've come to expect and have put strategies in place to manage the bad days better, I am always conscious of the bad days, and it causes me stress, which in turn, probably makes matters worse as the body when stressed releases the hormone cortisol.

Cortisol is the hormone that controls our flight or fight response and can have a negative impact on many vital functions of the body such as blood pressure and metabolism, but it also affects brain function and too much cortisol can inhibit the brain's ability to concentrate along with other negative effects such as low mood and anxiety. Not great when you are already feeling the pressure.

Many organisations test a person's ability to focus on a number of different tasks and prioritise work at recruitment stages of employment through competency-based questions and exercises, and during employment through performance reviews.

Whether you work in an office, a healthcare setting or service environment, we are all expected to own and deliver multiple tasks and it is unlikely that we will automatically be given the headspace to manage each task individually. As is shown by the respondents to the Pittsburgh survey on the most disruptive symptom of menopause, hot flushes were towards the bottom end of the list. Poor concentration was at the top and with good reason. It can feel very frightening to lose your ability to function effectively.

I asked my GP if he thought I was experiencing dementia my ability to think, and concentrate was so badly affected. He asked my age and reassured me following the standard dementia test that it was almost certainly menopause, but I had a very stressful few weeks with my imagination running away with me and struggling at work.

I was fascinated to know if there was a biological cause of poor concentration and if this was the case, what I could do about it. There are three main hormones at work in our body that are affected in menopause. When menopause begins its transition, oestrogen levels start to drop, and this can happen suddenly and significantly. Oestrogen is the hormone that connects everything up in our brains, helping one part connect to another. If oestrogen levels are fluctuating or dropping beneath certain levels, this will affect our brain's ability to function effectively and cause poor concentration and memory.

A study by scientists at the University of Pittsburgh in 2020 (1), found that cognitive performance declines with the loss of oestrogen. The part of the brain that is particularly affected is the frontal cortex, which is responsible for memory, problem solving, language, judgement, impulse control, and social behaviour. Not surprising then that struggling to draw down the word for something while having a conversation with someone who's name you can't remember is a thing in menopause. Also, important to note here, is that the study found that women who entered menopause through a transition phase, responded differently to oestrogen replacements that women who had had their ovaries removed, so if your menopause was surgical, and your body has had a sudden loss of oestrogen, it can have a massive impact very quickly.

Hormones and symptoms

Although I believe that I was already in the menopause transition before I had a hysterectomy, I had a surgical menopause because of endometriosis. My surgeon advised me to wait before resuming HRT to allow the endometriosis to die back (oestrogen causes endometriosis to grow). I spent a very distressing few months finding it very difficult to control my mood and resume my brain power. When I couldn't stand it anymore, I spoke to the surgeon who advised me to begin HRT again straight away. This made work was a very challenging time for me, and for other women I've seen in the same situation. It is particularly important for women to have access to specialist medical assessment and advice to help manage their symptoms.

Another of the menopause hormones testosterone is currently receiving a lot of press, and rightly so. Alice Smellie wrote in the Times (2) about the 'holy trinity of hormones', oestrogen, progesterone, and testosterone and the impact of a loss of testosterone on brain function causing brain fog. Women produce more testosterone that oestrogen, so the reduction has every bit as big an impact on our ability to feel well and function. If you have had a surgical menopause, your testosterone is halved. That is a huge change to your hormonal balance, and nobody told me that. The first I knew about it was when I saw menopause specialist nurse, Aly Dilks. Other than the loss of libido, testosterone isn't widely talked about in relation to menopause and as it isn't licensed for use with menopause, it can only be prescribed by a specialist. Testosterone as well as affecting libido, affects our levels of energy and low levels can lead to fatigue.

The third part of the trinity of hormones is progesterone. This is the hormone that during reproductive years, prepares the lining of the womb for an egg to embed and to maintain a pregnancy. Like oestrogen, progesterone declines during menopause and the loss of this particular hormone can disrupt periods causing them to be irregular and very heavy. Replacing a decline in progesterone can be a big help in reducing insomnia and encouraging sleep as well as some cognitive functions such as memory, as well as balancing mood, and reducing anxiety and depression.

If you've not been on the menopause journey, I'm probably not filling you with joy reading this, but I hope it gives you an idea of what many women experience and why it can be so hard to continue in the workplace while managing these symptoms. There are treatments that can make a huge difference to improving quality of life, but as with many treatments whether medical or homeopathic, what works for one woman, may not work for another and things change over time. Having a supportive workplace that can make some adjustments and provide access to specialist support is a critical piece of the jigsaw.

Referring to the top ten symptoms of menopause affecting work, identified by the University of Nottingham research, the table below lists the symptoms, possible impact in a work environment and options for adjustments.

Symptom	Impact	Solution
Poor concentration	Affects productivity which could lead to low self-esteem. Falling behind with work leading to increased stress and anxiety.	Provide quiet areas and hybrid working options.
Tiredness	Affects concentration, mood, increased chance of accidents. Increase in stress and anxiety.	Consider working patterns. Ensure rest breaks are available and happening. Provide access to employee assistance to support sleep and manage stress and anxiety.
Poor memory	Missing deadlines and completing tasks assigned to the worker. Not retaining information key to undertaking tasks.	Adjustments to manage workload. Software to manage reminders or Apps such as Microsoft To-Do, sticky note, reminders.
Feeling low/depressed	Lack of energy and motivation. Difficulties with concentration. Can cause problems with sleep.	Support through employee assistance programmes. Ability to talk openly with a supportive line manager. Support with workload. Flexible working.
Lowered confidence	Missing out on opportunities at work. Feelings of stress and anxiety.	Mentoring and coaching opportunities. Menopause employee groups and cafes.
Sleep disturbances	Low mood and depression. Affects ability to concentrate and increased stress and anxiety.	As with tiredness, consider working patterns. Ensure rest breaks are available and happening. Provide access to employee assistance to support sleep and manage stress and anxiety.
Irritability	Affects relationships and work and home, leading to low mood, stress, and anxiety.	Being able to have supportive conversations with line manager. Access to employee assistance programme. Coaching.
Hot flushes	Affects concentration, tiredness, feeling embarrassed.	Managing temperature in the work environment and providing easy access to fans. Considering fabric of uniforms. Hygienic washing facilities.
Joint & muscular aches	Pain can affect ability to sleep and concentrate and cause low mood and depression.	Review of workstation. Provide training on ergonomics. Provide ability to move around and suitable rest facilities.
Mood swings	Affects relationships and work and home and lead to depression.	Supportive line management and access to employee assistance programme. Ability to take rest breaks and support in managing stress.

All these symptoms can be unpleasant to experience and if you combine a number of them at any one time, they can be overwhelming. We are all different and are likely to experience symptoms differently and to different degrees depending on our circumstances. To be able to manage their symptoms in the workplace, women need to be treated as individuals. There needs to be a culture where honest and open discussions are encouraged and come from a place of support and without judgement.

In the next chapter I will cover rights and responsibilities in more detail, but it is important to note that many of the symptoms listed in the table above, could be considered to be a disability if they affect the individual for a longer period of time, and also affect their ability to carry out their normal duties. Reasonable adjustments, also discussed in more detail in the next chapter, should be considered carefully and regularly reviewed to ensure that the right support is being given. Menopause symptoms can fluctuate and change over time. For example, the cognitive ability that escaped me in the early years of my menopause transition has returned, but my hot flushes are on overdrive along with insomnia (and don't get me started on the snoring). Women can thrive during menopause with the right help from managers and the right working environment.

Actions for employers

- Consider how the work environment can affect women with menopause symptoms.
- Educate line managers in how to have empathetic conversations and offer support.
- Educate managers and colleagues in menopause and menopause symptoms, and how they might impact women in the workplace.

Chapter 6

Knowing menopause rights and responsibilities

Despite the size of the population affected by menopause at work, very few countries have specific legislation in place to support and protect menopausal women in the workplace. An article in Euronews Next (1), reported on the lack of workplace menopause legislation such as menopause leave anywhere in the world. Despite this a number of countries including Spain, Indonesia, Japan, South Korea and Taiwan are introducing menstrual leave, a positive and much needed step.

A report written on behalf of the UK Government published in July 2022, 'Menopause and the Workplace' (2), highlights how critical it is to keep women of menopause age in a depleted workforce, not least of all because they are the fastest growing demographic already in the workforce. However, the authors of the report recognise that to do this, there has to be a vast change to stop women leaving in droves. People Management Magazine reported in June 2021 (3) that there was an increase in cases in the UK Employment Tribunal citing menopause of 44%, on the previous year, with an increase of 75% in cases mentioning menopause on the previous year. The legal jurisdiction for the cases fell mainly under disability discrimination, followed closely by sex discrimination.

What this shows is that while there is legislation in the UK (and potentially other countries who have embedded equality legislation) that offers protection, it is not clear where menopause fits in. This could be confusing not only for women who believe they have been treated less favourably, but also for employers understanding their responsibilities and in making this clear to the managers and staff who operationalise this in the workplace.

Confusion and uncertainty are never helpful and under these circumstances not ideal in reassuring the women whose knowledge and skills we want to retain. If you have read up to this point and are thinking so what if they don't stay, I recommend you re-read Chapter 2 on menopause and how it impacts the workplace for both a moral and economic case.

So where does this leave us? The UK Government report, 'Menopause and the Workplace' (2) has set out a number of recommendations including:

- The appointment of a Menopause Ambassador to champion good practice;
- The Government role modelling best practice menopause policies;

- Specific leave to prevent women being 'forced out of work by insensitive and rigid sickness policies'; and
- The commencement of a yet to be enacted part of the Equalities Act 2010 which would allow dual discrimination claims as well as adding menopause to the nine existing protected characteristics covered by the Act.

With the voice of menopausal women becoming much louder in the workplace, it remains to be seen if any of the recommendations in the report become a reality, but in case you are wondering if there is a need for protection from discrimination or robust policies and education, have a look at the voices of menopausal women shared in the survey that feeds into the report:

> *'I needed to know that I wouldn't be penalised for my symptoms'.*

'A lot of derogatory terms for a menopausal woman in her 50's, such as moody cow, grumpy, stupid, and ones I can't remember off the top of my head.'

'Reinforced stereotypes of middle-aged women being forgetful and unreliable.'

'Being older… it definitely ended my career progression'

In summary, the report recommends a number of key actions that will assist women to remain in the workplace:

1. Health
   - The roll out of a major health campaign with communications targeted at GPs on changes to HRT prescriptions.
   - A commitment by the Government to scrap dual prescription charges for oestrogen and progesterone.

- Menopause is a mandatory part of continuing professional development for GPs.
- A menopause specialist in every Clinical Commissioning Group area by 2024.

2. The Workplace
    - The Government role models good practice by ensuring that there are menopause policies across the Civil Service.
    - Trialing menopause leave.
    - The creation of a menopause ambassador.

3. The Law
    - The commencement of Section of the Equality Act (2010) that allows dual discrimination claims based on several protected characteristics.

- Consider making menopause a protected characteristic.

These recommendations would provide both the necessary health support and protection for women in the workplace and would be a big step in the right direction towards making menopause an integral part of our policies and culture, with the right medical interventions in place to enable the continuation of work.
In the next section, we'll look at existing rights. While I have outlined UK specific rights, there is broadly similar legislation in place across Europe and North America. **This section is not intended to replace legal advice, which should always be sought in advance of any actions taken.**

Rights

If you are in the UK, protection comes from two sources, The Equality Act (2010) and Health and Safety at Work Act (1974). The Equality Act provides protection against discrimination and the Health and Safety at Work Act, protects workers health, safety, and welfare.

The Equality Act 2010

The Equality Act names nine specific characteristics that are covered within the Act, and where menopause is concerned, there are four characteristics that are relevant:

- sex
- disability
- age
- gender reassignment

ACAS (Arbitration, Conciliation Advisory Service) provides a very clear outline of where employers and their workers could discriminate against menopausal women. (4)

Sex - treating someone differently because of their sex could be considered discrimination. For example, overlooking a woman for promotion because of concerns that her menopause symptoms might prevent her from carrying out the required duties would be discriminatory.

Disability - the definition of a disability under the Equality Act is 'a physical or mental impairment that has a 'substantial' and 'long-term' negative effect on your ability to do normal daily activities'. The definition could mean that menopause, or some menopause symptoms could be considered a disability. Workers have the right to not be discriminated against, and employers have a responsibility to make reasonable adjustments and to reduce or remove disadvantages.

Age - Menopause affects women at particular age so disadvantages affecting this group could be perceived as age discrimination. However, as ACAS point out, younger women could be affected as well, but making comments about a woman's age in relation to menopause has the potential to be discriminatory.

Gender reassignment - anyone with a female reproductive system will experience menopause, and ACAS highlight the importance of being aware that this may also apply to transgender people and people transitioning.

Health and safety duty of care
Employers in the UK should also consider their responsibilities under Management of Health and Safety at Work Regulations 1999 (MHSWR) which includes identifying groups of employees whose health and safety may be more at risk and carrying out suitable assessments of those risks.

A risk assessment is an important part of protecting menopausal women but also gaining a better understanding of how symptoms can affect work performance. It takes the responsibility away from individual women and places it with the employer to resolve. This is a vital step forward in moving away from the stereotype of menopausal women as incapable.

I have provided a menopause risk assessment template in the resources section of this book.

Case Law

As I have said throughout this book, I hope that you will consider it perfectly reasonable to support menopausal women in the workplace, but I recognise that there will be employers who may think that it's not necessary or don't understand how their actions could be perceived as discriminatory or treating a menopausal woman less favourably. I've included the headlines of some prominent case law in the UK Employment Tribunal Service.

Merchant vs BTplc

In this case, Ms Merchant had received a final written warning for her performance and was subsequently dismissed by her manager. Her manager was aware that she was experiencing menopause symptoms which included struggling with her concentration, however, he dismissed Ms Merchant without carrying out any further medical investigations.

The tribunal upheld Ms Merchant's claim of sex discrimination and unfair dismissal on the grounds that he wouldn't have taken this approach with other conditions that specifically affect women. In other words, a man wouldn't have been treated the same way.

A vs Bonmarche Ltd

A's manager used demeaning language about her in front of her (younger) colleagues, including calling her a dinosaur. She was criticised for making mistakes, and he refused to adjust the temperature in the shop. Up until she began her menopause transition, A had been a high achiever and had been with the company for 37 years. She had complained to

management about her treatment, but no action was taken which led to her going off sick. When she returned to work, she was victimised by her manager.
A successfully claimed age and sex discrimination.

Donnachie vs Telent Technology Solutions Ltd.
Ms Donnachie is an important case in relation to considering whether menopause is classified as a disability in the eyes of the law, and in this case the judge ruled that it could be considered a disability. Ms Donnachie experienced numerous hot flushes throughout the day which were accompanied by other significant symptoms, palpitations and anxiety. Her employer had tried to argue that as her symptoms were typical menopause symptoms, they did not affect her significantly. The judge ruled in Ms Donnachie's favour saying, "I see no reason why, in principle, 'typical' menopausal symptoms cannot have the

relevant disabling effect on an individual." Something that anyone who has ever suffered with hot flushes, or any of the other joyful menopause symptoms, will no doubt agree with.

As mentioned earlier in the book, the courts are recognising not only the effects menopause has on women in the workplace, but upholding claims by employees of discrimination.

Good practice

So, what does good practice look like for employers when it comes to supporting menopausal women? In summary, it looks like this:

- Educate your workers on menopause in the same way you would for other protected characteristics. Use of language, treatment, support, having conversations. (Covered in more detail in the next chapter).

- Don't demean women because of their symptoms or treat them less favourably.
- Consider and make adjustments to help with symptoms, such as flexible working, location of work.
- Look at your sickness policy and make sure that it doesn't impose unreasonable outcomes for women who are struggling to manage menopause symptoms.
- Involve occupational health professionals in understanding the impact of symptoms and making adjustments.
- Develop policies that allow for flexibility and ensure respect for colleagues.
- Provide resources that educate colleagues on menopause, support

menopausal women and signpost them clearly.

- Have honest and open conversations about menopause and reduce the stigma.

Making Adjustments

ACAS describes reasonable adjustments as doing something that will remove the disadvantage to a person with a disability. Adjustments should be about getting the best out of the employee and supporting them.

Don't spend time on working out if this is a disability or not, far better to spend the time on what adjustments could be put in place to help them. Ideally if you have occupational health use them. This can be arranged through an outsourced company and does not need to be in-house. Carrying out a risk assessment will help you to understand what could happen to make the workplace better for the employee and is part of the employer's duty of care in the UK.

The CIPD, a professional body for HR practitioners, recommends treating menopausal women in the same way as anyone who has a long-term health condition, which would include making reasonable adjustments to help manage symptoms. (5) They also advise that menopause should be included in health and sickness absence policies which would help managers and workers to see clearly how menopause is positioned in the organisation.

Menopause affects people in very different ways so adjustments should always be tailored to the needs of the individual and ideally with the support of an occupational health professional. Symptoms can change over time so a review should always be carried out as and when the individual experiences changing symptoms and reviewed every 12 months or less if symptoms change.

Holding a conversation about reasonable adjustments:

Step 1 - ideally refer the worker to an occupational health professional who can discuss the individual's symptoms and the impact on their ability to carry out their duties.

Step 2 - meet with the worker to discuss the results and recommendations of the assessment and agree with the worker what will be put in to place to support them.

Step 3 - agree a follow update to review and check that the adjustments are providing the anticipated support.

Step 4 - confirm in writing what has been agreed and the review dates.

Possible adjustments could include:

- Flexible working (shift pattern, part time working)
- Work location
- Accessible parking space
- Ventilation
- Location of workstation (natural light, quiet area)
- Adjustments to uniform
- Support with workload

Sickness absence

Workers may feel uncomfortable about reporting sickness absence because of tough sickness management procedures. Employers will have to consider their culture carefully. Not only could it be difficult for women to be open about menopause symptoms and the impact, but it is also very important to educate managers to see menopause as a long-term health condition. The length of time menopause affects women and the extent of the symptoms for many women, means that they could find themselves caught up in a punitive sickness absence management procedure very quickly. However, with the right approach to reasonable adjustments and occupational health support, many absences can be prevented.

The CIPD in their excellent guide to menopause at work for HR professionals (5) recommend adding menopause as a reason for absence which then allows it to be managed through a more appropriate procedure than the procedure for persistent short-term absences. Their view is that if the symptoms affect capacity to work (which for many women they do) then it's the right thing to do to treat menopause outside short term persistent absence procedures, and instead support absence in the same way as a long-term health condition would be managed.

With all of this, expertise is needed to ensure that the right decisions are made to get the right outcomes. In researching this chapter, it was refreshing to see that guidance was focused on supporting women rather than strict management procedures. From personal experience and the experience of the many women I have spoken to about menopause at work, it is possible to thrive and work successfully with the right support framework and a culture of understanding and respect.

Actions for employers

- Rework sickness absence policies and procedures to explicitly mention how menopause is managed to avoid confusion and misunderstandings
- Carry out menopause risk assessments
- Train managers in have conversation about menopause
- Educate workforce on menopause

Tools

- Menopause risk assessment (in Resources Chapter)

Chapter 7

Education, education, education

My experience of learning

When I started my menopause transition, I knew very little about the symptoms or my options for treatment. I'm quite a long way through that journey and I'm still learning. I can remember being in a meeting with my boss, and she asked me what I wanted to talk about. I sat for a few minutes, and I could feel the panic rising as I couldn't remember why I was there. It felt as though my brain was empty.

Very few people around me were talking about menopause. My lack of knowledge about menopause, made me think that I might be experiencing the early stages of dementia. It was far too long after my symptoms started that I began to realise that what I was feeling could be menopause. There were some very helpful conversations, but some that reinforced the unhelpful myths. One such myth was that HRT just delayed menopause so by using it, you were just putting off the inevitable. Far better to power through it now and get it out of the way!

This kind of misinformation shows how important education is not only to colleagues and managers, but to women themselves. Information from an experienced and qualified and menopause practitioner is a vital part of women getting the right treatment for their individual symptoms and bodies - one size most definitely does not fit all.

The first stage has to be providing information for women who are experiencing (or will experience) perimenopause or menopause. Reducing the myths and providing good quality information is a vital part of reducing the stigma of menopause and creating a culture where menopausal women can thrive. Most organisations will have an intranet or SharePoint site where information can be stored, or you could signpost to an external provider. Either way, set up a knowledge hub for resources and signposting.

Knowledge Hub

A knowledge hub is a location (usually digital) where an organisation can provide information. It could also provide the opportunity to exchange information (think Facebook groups), but this would need to be monitored and moderated so will need to be resourced by someone in your organisation to avoid misinformation.

The information about menopause that would be helpful might include:

- The symptoms of menopause and how they affect women and what is happening to their bodies.
- What treatment is available (but **not** medical advice).

- How to access that treatment.
- What support your organisation provides menopausal women, and how to access it.

Asking women what they would find helpful would be a great starting point for kicking off the conversation about menopause in the workplace. Make sure that the information you provide is provided by a reputable source.

There are many resources available that provide resources both for individuals and for organisations, which saves you the job of starting from scratch. I've listed a few of my favourites with a description of what they are and who they are aimed at:

Let's all talk menopause - an online programme of talks from experts and clinicians that provides information on everything from HRT to anxiety, sleep and brain fog and includes a live question and answer session. Speakers can be provided including Mariella

Frostrup, Alice Smellie and experts on menopause subjects. Individual and corporate packages available.
https://www.letsalltalkmenopause.co.uk/

Simply Menopausal - run by experienced menopause nurse practitioner Aly Dilks, who is also a member of the British Menopause Society. Aly provides online and in person consultations and can prescribe. Individual and corporate packages available.
https://www.simplymenopausal.co.uk/

Balance - A website and app from Dr Louise Newson, that provides information on menopause with a menopause library containing medically approved content. Individual and corporate packages available.
https://www.balance-menopause.com/

Daisy Network - An organisation that supports women who have POI (Premature Ovarian Insufficiency) which is a condition where the

ovaries aren't working properly meaning that the lack of oestrogen, progesterone, and testosterone (produced by the ovaries) lead to menopause symptoms at an early age affecting 1 in 100 women. Daisy Network is a charity that provides information and support to women with the condition.
https://www.daisynetwork.org/

Many organisations find it helpful to develop a policy to frame the company's point of view on managing menopause in the workplace.

Developing a policy

I have a love/hate relationship with policies. I love clear, simple, concise policies written in plain English. I hate, well, the opposite. For a policy to be used, and to add any value to an organisation it should be accessible to as many people as possible through language and tone and have a purpose. I'm not a fan of writing a policy for the sake of it - not everything needs to be a policy.

In the case of menopause, my perspective is that having a policy is a useful tool in setting out the organisation's point of view on menopause and providing guidance on roles and responsibilities in managing menopause in the workplace. This can help to reduce confusion about who does what, when and set out the organisation's expectations on how managers support menopausal workers.

A menopause policy might include sections on:

- Who the policy is aimed at
- Information about menopause, symptoms, how these symptoms might manifest at work
- Roles and responsibilities - who should do what and when
- What support the organisation offers menopausal women and where to find it
- Examples of adjustments for the symptoms

- Links to other policies such as absence, equality, and diversity
- Signpost to other information and resources

Many organisations and workers that are employed globally and employ people from different cultures. When describing what menopause is and the symptoms, using terminology from the relevant culture helps to foster understanding. There is evidence that women in different cultures may experience menopause symptoms differently, so it is important not to make generalisations.

A Google search will usually bring up a number of menopause policies you could use for inspiration. Dr Louise Newson's Balance provides a menopause policy template that can be tailored to the style and tone of voice of your organisation. https://balance-menopause.com/uploads/2022/03/Menopause-Policy-and-Guidance-FINAL.pdf

We've noted throughout the book that menopause has carried a stigma for years which can make it a subject that managers find difficult to talk about with their workers. There may be a number of reasons for this, including a lack of understanding about menopause, worrying about saying the wrong things, or managing cultural nuances. This is where providing guidelines for managers is invaluable.

Manager guidelines

The CIPD the UK's professional organisation for HR practitioners, provides a downloadable guide for managers of people which they have developed with contributions from BUPA.
The guide includes:

- Why it's important to support women during the menopause transition
- A detailed description of menopause and menopause symptoms

- The role of a line manager
- How to have honest and open conversations
- How to carry out a menopause risk assessment
- Making reasonable adjustments for symptoms
- Managing performance positively
- Resources

It's a comprehensive guide for managers and can easily be tailored to the tone of voice your organisation uses for its communication materials, and specific cultural aspects. (1) https://www.cipd.co.uk/Images/line-manager-guide-to-menopause_tcm18-95174.pdf

Other online resources include a great guide from ACAS to how to have a conversation about menopause with an employee here https://www.acas.org.uk/menopause-at-work/talking-with-staff-about-the-menopause

Access to a written document, however comprehensive, is not the total solution, and as human beings we learn in different ways. Having the opportunity to connect with a group of people around the organisation who have been trained in managing menopause in the workplace, is an ideal way of keeping the conversation going and reducing the stigma. Enter Menopause Mentors.

Menopause Mentors

Menopause is a subject not everyone feels comfortable discussing with their line manager. Women may want to discuss how to have a conversation about their menopause symptoms with an independent person who can help them to frame the conversation before it takes place. Developing a group of people across the organisation to take on this role, provides a network of people trained in understanding menopause and the organisations menopause resources and support framework. It is important to be clear that Menopause Mentors should not be providing medical advice or counselling. This should only be provided by clinicians and in the right circumstances. The role of a Menopause Mentor should be to:

- Educate on menopause, the symptoms, and how symptoms can affect women in the workplace.
- Facilitator of resources for menopause, signposting to policies, guidelines, and wellbeing
- Change agent advocating menopausal women and through conversations and education, helping to reduce the stigma of menopause and raising awareness
- Advising and guiding managers and colleagues in having conversations, carrying out risk assessments and in some cases, possible adjustments to work to manage symptoms

Summary

Education is a key part of providing an inclusive and accessible workplace to women, trans and non-binary workers and retaining them in the workplace. The more we all understand about menopause and its impact on the workplace, the more we will reduce stigma and help a large and growing part of the workplace to thrive.

Actions for employers

- Create a knowledge hub of resources for workers experiencing menopause and managers and colleagues.
- Develop a policy to set out the organisation's perspective on menopause and a framework for support
- Develop guidelines for managers on supporting menopausal workers

- Set up and train a network of menopause mentors who can advise on internal resources and policies.

Chapter 8

Performance management

Performance management is one of those topics that generates a lot of heated discussion. To hold appraisals, not to hold appraisals? How is reward linked to performance? Performance ratings and who gets what? It can be a complex and controversial subject, even without the dynamics that menopause brings into the conversation. I'll propose and discuss a definition for performance management so that we have a common starting point, but before I do that, I want to set out a perspective on how organisations and their line managers should view the menopause and managing performance.

Menopause and managing performance - a perspective

Much of the guidance on managing menopause, and academic literature on menopause at work, focuses on a medical approach to menopause, in essence, approaching the management of menopause at work as disease and disability, using occupational health advice as a scaffold for the reasonable adjustments that will be put in place to make things right for menopausal women. Some women reject the idea of being pigeonholed as having a disability as they fear that this will add to the additional bias and view that they lack the capability to carry out their roles. I can see the point of view, and this is a tricky one to call. In a workplace environment where there is so little education about menopause, line managers are often lacking in information and nervous about doing the wrong thing. Having a framework to support women would provide a well-established process for understanding and managing symptoms in the workplace. A disability/reasonable adjustments policy and process is a helpful resource to support managers in having a discussion that they may be nervous about. Many menopause symptoms are medical, so until there is a specific legal structure that recognises menopause as a protected characteristic, following this existing disability support pathway is the right thing to do.

However, an article on menopause and the workplace that sets out an agenda for HR research (1), suggesting that providing adjustments to manage symptoms is only one half of the story. They propose that for women to thrive at work during menopause there needs to be a 'two-way relationship between menopause and work'. What this means is that symptoms make working difficult, but conversely, circumstances in the workplace could make symptoms worse. The implications for employers and managers the authors argue, is that culture is hugely important in making the workplace a viable option for women during the menopause transition. We'll look at this in more detail in Chapter 10 but keep this at the front of your mind when you are reading this chapter and considering your actions and discussions in the workplace: circumstances in the workplace, can make symptoms worse.

Performance management what is it, and how does it affect women in the workplace

The UK's professional HR body, the CIPD, describes performance management as a series of activities that are designed to deliver value from what the employee creates.

> *'At its best, performance management centres on two-way discussion and regular, open and supportive feedback on progress towards objectives. It*

brings together many principles that enable good people management practice, including learning and development, performance measurement and organisational development.' (2)

This description positions performance management as a positive joint activity designed to support workers, rather than a punitive activity. Using this description, and building the activities highlighted here, it would be a perfectly natural thing to do to ask, 'what do you need to be able to do your job better?' As well as the skills, and knowledge we need to be able to perform our roles, why not add in environmental factors such as a quiet space when we have difficulty concentrating, not being overloaded workwise, and not booking in breakfast meetings if we are experiencing insomnia?

When menopause is weaved into discussions and supporting symptoms are just another part of what else managers can do to enable performance, it becomes a less invasive and more enabling discussion.

Of course, all of this depends on the relationship with line managers and their attitude towards menopause. Normalising discussions about menopause in the workplace becomes even more critical, as does recognising menopause and menopause symptoms and the impact. Where women don't feel confident to have the conversation, it is possible to provide other channels if line manager conversations not possible. This could be through a network of Menopause Champions or Occupational Health or HR.

The advantage of developing a network of Menopause Champions is that this is a group that can be specifically trained in menopause and may well have experienced menopause themselves, helping them to have a deeper understanding of the impact of menopause. Though of course, allyship (an advocate on behalf of a group of people that are marginalised) is also invaluable and hugely important to inclusion.

Case study - Helen's story

> *Helen is a senior manager in the marketing function of a UK based company. She recalls how successful her career had been, even while managing it alongside having a family. Her colleagues saw her as a critical part of the team, and often sought her out when there were complex problems to be solved. Helen had the ability to see the bigger picture and take lots of complex information and sort it into actions and solutions.*

In her personal life, Helen was finding it increasingly difficult to manage alongside her role, with growing anxiety, sleepless nights caused by insomnia and made worse by the anxiety, and exhaustion. Still in her mid-forties, Helen had considered the menopause transition as a possible cause, and had visited her GP for a blood test, only to be told that she wasn't 'menopausal'. As her depression grew, her workload had increased, and she was finding it difficult to manage at work. Brain fog meant that the problem-solving skills she was valued for were depleted at critical moments, and the situation came to a head, when she was presenting in an important meeting and wasn't able to articulate what she wanted to say, forgot key facts and figures and had a hot flush that exacerbated an already difficult situation.

After the meeting, Helen's boss asked to speak to her to have a debrief of the meeting. She wasn't able to make sense of what had happened during the meeting and could feel tears of frustration and humiliation welling up. Her boss paused the meeting to allow Helen time to compose herself. The meeting continued later in the day at which time, Helen's boss told her that she had consulted with HR about concerns she had regarding Helen's performance, in particular, that Helen did not seem able to manage her workload and that the quality of her work, was suffering, she didn't seem as engaged with the team as she had been, and that she had appeared unprepared for the meeting where she had struggled with her presentation. There was even mention of a Performance Improvement Plan.

Helen was devastated and more so because she couldn't understand what was happening to her. None of her friends were in the menopause transition, and it wasn't a subject discussed at work, and there were no resources available. She made an appointment with her GP and was able to get an appointment relatively quickly with a GP she hadn't seen before.

The new GP recognised straight away that Helen was showing symptoms of menopause transition and following an analysis of her hormone levels, prescribed HRT and the Mirena Coil to alleviate her symptoms. She began to feel that her symptoms improved, slowly but steadily, and her work had returned for the most part, to its normal levels. Understanding the underlying cause of her problems, and likely triggers for symptoms, Helen was able to work with her boss to make the adjustments necessary.

As a side note, Helen's boss is now in the menopause transition and has been able to use the learning she gained from her interactions with Helen, to consider the support she needs from her boss, and to lobby their employers for more education and resources.

In the case study, Helen's 'capability' is being called into question by her manager and there is a suggestion of her being put into a management process that could result in her receiving some kind of management action. This is inappropriate on many levels. As we saw in the chapter on rights and responsibilities, menopausal women have a double, triple whammy when it comes to how they are viewed (gender, age, disability and in some cases gender reassignment). Where a number of characteristics cross over this is known as intersectionality and employers could face penalties for less favourable treatment resulting from one of these characteristics.

The authors of the report I reference earlier in this chapter, (1) point to research on pregnancy that shows that the reproductive activities of women are seen as an inconvenience. We have periods and associated conditions that cause us to have time off. We have babies, maybe intrusive infertility treatment and then to cap it all off we go through menopause. In my career in HR, I have had to challenge the views that women's reproductive lives are inconvenient to work. Personally, having experienced all of these, I think we've taken one for the team and deserve a massive pat on the back to keep going during all of this, certainly not being performance managed for perceived capability issues.

By now, you'll probably have guessed my point of view on this. Women have reproductive functions, periods, babies, menopause. We need to get over it and get on with it. Women have huge value to the workplace and with the right understanding and approach, the effects of the additional challenges we face can be managed.

Taking a positive approach to performance management by enabling an environment where individuals can thrive, creates good performance and loyalty. I know many people who stay with their employers in the face of being poached by competitors, because they want to stay with an employer that values them and supports them. It's 101 employee engagement.

So, in summary, performance management should be a two-way relationship where a line manager helps to create a working environment that enables the employee to perform well. This might be through flexible working, being mindful of the timings of meetings, or not excessively overloading employees with work.

Women who are experiencing menopause symptoms that are affecting their work, should not be placed into punitive processes, but supported in accessing the right treatment from their GP or any employee resources provided by the employer and adjustments made. Remember that the working environment could be making the symptoms worse.

Actions for employers

- Educate managers on how adverse menopause symptoms might affect performance, and how to support performance in this situation.

Chapter 9
Opportunity and promotion during menopause

For most women, menopause happens at a time in their careers when they have developed high levels of experience and expertise. They are likely to have been in the workplace for over twenty years and may well hold senior positions.

A report published on 2021 by Standard Chartered and the Financial Services Skills Commission highlighted what a serious problem menopause is causing to retaining women in the industry. (1) This and other reports quote women who feel marginalised in their roles by age, or their fear that their menopause symptoms will limit their ability to do their jobs well enough. Women interviewed for the research shared their concerns, that having spent much of their careers having to compete with men for promotion, often while juggling caring responsibilities, they now felt that they were now having to compete with younger women as well. Eventually this becomes exhausting and takes considerable resilience to keep trying. Imagine also adding into the mix being a woman of colour and up against colour bias as well? Intersectionality, where a number of characteristics crossover, such as gender, age, ethnicity for example, adds a whole new and challenging dimension to managing a career.

Importantly, one of the key findings was that women can stay in work and progress with the right support. Earlier in this book, I highlighted the skills gap in many industries and the economic need to retain women in the workplace both at individual level and for organisations. The Standard Chartered Report (1) uses data from McKinsey that found that companies with a diverse executive board had above average profitability compared to those without. Diversity makes a positive difference to the success of organisations.

In the previous chapter, we discussed performance and how menopause affects performance. The Standard Chartered report refers to women losing confidence in their abilities at work because of increased anxiety, being less able to concentrate, and general brain fog. The report presents this information in a broader context by pointing out that menopause is a temporary state and that women often come out of the other side of menopause even stronger. Furthermore, all of these symptoms can be managed through relatively minor adjustments to working life such as flexible working, taking breaks when symptoms flair and managing their workload around times of the day when the symptoms may be worse.

Suki's story

It was four years after my hysterectomy before I was offered HRT. The symptoms were terrible, and it affected my confidence, filling me with self-doubt.

Before I started taking HRT, I can remember numerous conversations with my manager about applying for a promotion. I was also on secondment and promotion was one of my goals in my development plan, but I felt I couldn't do it with menopause symptoms. I questioned my abilities and felt my processing was much slower than prior to menopause.

As time went on, I felt able to discuss how I was feeling with my manager, and a few select individuals. I found a great support network in the workplace and another manager in the business who I would describe as a male ally (someone who actively supports and promotes people from underrepresented groups). They supported me in opening up the conversation with my wider team about how menopause was affecting me. Without their support I would have been frightened to open up about it to the team, many of whom were a younger demographic and male. It opened up the dialogue and built awareness. It was one of those reflection moments but helped colleagues to understand the impact. The support from the team afterwards was amazing.

I'm so glad I was able to open up about how menopause was affecting me. I wanted my colleagues to know that it wasn't that I'm not a capable individual, it was the menopause that was affecting me. I know that my team has my back and will step in if I need them to.

Suki's story reflects the experience of many of the women I talk to about menopause in the workplace. There is a fear of opening up to managers and colleagues about what is happening to them in case they are treated less favourably. The other side of that fear is that they may be judged as incompetent if what is happening to them isn't recognised and acknowledged as 'real' and a temporary state that can be managed and mitigated with the right support and adjustments.

Promotion and career

So, what impact does menopause have on women seeking promotion? The Standard Chartered report tells us that a significant number of women were less likely to seek promotion because of their symptoms, and the reason given was that they were concerned that they would not be able to perform because of their menopause symptoms or they were concerned about being judged. While there is research that shows that certain aspects of work can change during menopause, (2) there is also evidence that with the right adjustments and support from employers, there is far less impact on performance, and in fact, performance can be enhanced greatly following menopause.

If the evidence is that performance can be managed well by putting in place adjustments, and if there is also evidence that women's performance can be even better following the menopause transition, why are women still stepping away from the workplace and stepping down from managerial roles during menopause?

It's clear both from the reports I've cited and women I've spoken to, that support is key, but a major barrier is the fear of being judged at a time when they are already feeling vulnerable, and anxiety is increased. Typically, older workers experience negative stereotypes around capability, but the stereotypes are considerably worse for women (3). Sometimes this can be in the form of assumptions about an individual's career aspirations, or in the form of teasing about brain fog and hot flushes.

What women want

When I started researching this chapter my search terms were women career midlife. The majority of results were about career changes. It took me a couple of pages to get to anything not related to changing careers in midlife, and it was the same for academic peer review journals. Now I don't have a scientifically robust research base for this, but it does make you wonder if the results are so skewed towards changing careers, that many women have just had enough by this stage in their careers, and they are looking for something that they can balance with their menopause symptoms. Women still have caring responsibilities in late career. They are having babies in their forties and caring for elderly parents. It's easy to see why it could be tempting to change careers to something that allows you to keep all these balls in the air especially if you are not feeling supported at work.

An article on midlife career transitions highlights the challenges experienced by women of both dealing with fluctuating hormones and the impact of harmful stereotypes, branding us as weak, unpredictable, emotional and incompetent. (4) Sound familiar? If these are the labels attached to us it's no wonder, we lose confidence and self-esteem, choosing to step back rather that apply for promotions and develop our careers.

At this stage in their careers, women and men are often reassessing their identity and re-evaluating their careers. (4) For many women, it's the start of a new freedom from their reproductive lives (pregnancy, fertility treatment, periods). Remember the grandmother hypothesis? Hormones are disruptive and when we finally get them under control, we are bigger, better and stronger. Much of this however is at the mercy of our workplace environment and culture. If menopausal women are subjected to negative stereotypes and a lack of adjustments and support, why would they stay engaged with their employer and work in general?

What can we do to help women wanting to grow their careers?

There is much more recognition that carers need flexibility to balance home and life, and this has been embedded in legislation across many countries in Europe for many years now. Flexibility needs to continue even into senior roles, allowing women to manage their symptoms and their careers. This is much easier to achieve where there are women role models. Being able to look at senior leaders and see someone who looks like them, shows them that menopausal women are valuable and necessary. Speaking openly about our journeys also shows that senior women leaders are human beings that get menopausal symptoms. I am very grateful to a senior woman who shared with me her experience of endometriosis and menopause and how she had to manage flooding and the pain in a very male environment. Those stories help us to see that you have value and are capable, even if your body is being a massive pain in the butt.

Women often have another career setback if they have taken a career break to have children. In addition to the negative menopause stereotypes, they may also be perceived to be behind other younger women and men because of the time they took out of the workplace to raise children, particularly if they are in a more junior management position in the organisation.

Organisations need to move away from the time served approach to promotion and focus much more on strengths and potential when reviewing talent. If you are balancing caring responsibilities, career, menopause, the chances are you have a ton of resilience and many valuable skills. Leadership isn't always about traditional upward career pathways.

Louise Hymers founder of the Menopause Matters affinity group at PwC says, 'I felt that menopause had stalled my career and impacted my work negatively. Starting the menopause group, I've felt much more confident and empowered in my career.' Louise leads a thriving menopause employee group that is hugely valued and has achieved great changes for the menopausal women it supports. That is leadership right there.

Women mentoring other women

I'm a massive fan of affinity groups. Finding your tribe and having somewhere that you can share your experience without the fear of being judged is an important part of feeling included. Marcella Allison and Laura Gale share their thoughts on a group mentoring model called 'network-based mentoring' which was developed by Dr Kerry Ann Rockquemore. (5) Rather than happy a top-down method of mentoring, mentees are encouraged to identify mentors are from a group, rather than an individual (often restricted by the time pressures of senior execs) to fulfill the list of what they need from the mentoring relationship to grow their careers. Where the members of the group have either experienced menopause or are a menopause ally (man or woman) this provides an additional layer of understanding.

Summary

At the end of the penultimate chapter, there is a clear theme emerging. Menopause for many women can be very challenging, especially when combined with work and the other responsibilities we have in our lives. Creating a culture when menopause is a normal part of our working lives provides the foundations for everything else, we've covered in the previous chapters,

Actions for employers

- Establish a menopause affinity group
- Review promotion criteria focusing on strengths and potential (and not on time served)

- Consider flexible working as an option for senior managers and leaders
- Create a network of mentors trained in supporting menopausal women and careers

Chapter 10

A culture where menopausal women thrive

Reflecting on what I've learned from women about menopause at work, both as an HR practitioner and from writing this book, it struck me how much the culture of an organisation can impact their experience of working with menopause. The culture sets the tone for the how the whole organisation responds to menopausal women, but culture can be an amorphous word so understanding what it is and why it's important is a good place to start.

What is culture?

The phrase 'the way we do things around here' is often used to describe culture. As with national culture, organisation culture has common characteristics like language, values, and beliefs and even dress. The way we think, and feel can be influenced by our groups in the workplace (1) so how the organisation positions menopause has a ripple effect, and that ripple effect can be positive or negative. When an organisation doesn't talk about menopause or it is stigmatised, that frame of mind can pervade throughout the organisation.

Integrating menopause into normal workplace culture can be mapped by using a model of organisational culture. Here I've adapted a famous model developed by Edgar Schein in the 1980s (2) to illustrate how to bring a culture to life.

There were three layers to Schein's model:
1. Underlying beliefs about the organisation and the way things are done.
2. Values that are openly talked about and shape the way things are done.
3. The artefacts or visible things that show what an organisation is all about.

Relating this to the approach to menopause in an organisation, it might look something like this:

1. Underlying beliefs - With many organisations, their values and beliefs are so deeply ingrained that it's not talked about in the same way. For example, I worked for IKEA, and we were all very clear that IKEA stood for anyone whatever a customer's position in life, being able to have good quality stylish furniture at an affordable price with minimal impact on the environment. That social conscience was visible and a big part of many employees choosing to work for IKEA. The gender and age demographics of a workplace give an indication of whether it's an organisation where middle aged women want to work. How an organisation supports its workers and appears in public in the press, give an impression of its underlying beliefs.

2. Values - The second layer, or values layer is much more visible, and most organisations share their values internally and often externally to potential recruits, customers and suppliers. This also sets the tone for behaviours in an organisation. But beware. Organisations that don't live up to their values will see their employees heading out of the door in the blink of an eye.

3. The artefacts are the easiest to see and you will probably be familiar with many of these things and have some of them in your workplace. You might have lanyards with 'menopause ally' on them. You might reward someone for their work in supporting their menopausal colleagues at an awards ceremony. Workshops, online learning, posters and postcards are visible ways of bringing menopause awareness to life. Telling stories about how menopause has affected women in the workplace or has been supported is a vital part of embedding open discussion about menopause in the culture. This might be in an online video, in a team meeting or through a newsletter.

Some organisations may think that their culture is menopause friendly, but this may not always be the case. To truly create a culture that is inclusive, understand how employees see the culture of their workplace. Do menopausal women feel included in the workplace and do their colleagues and managers feel sufficiently educated to support them would be a good basis for developing an understanding. This can be done in a number of ways which could include a culture specific survey, interviews or focus groups.

By doing this, not only do employers understand their culture, but they are involving employees in creating the right culture. As discussed earlier in the book, menopause is experienced in different ways by different people. The women themselves, colleagues, and managers. Assumptions and generalisations can't be made and shouldn't be made and being given a voice and having that voice listened to is a key factor in employee engagement.

if organisations have cultures where menopause is hidden, and stigmatised true inclusion of menopausal women is unlikely. Of course, other groups in the workplace may also lack trust in an organisation that is not truly inclusive of marginalised groups of colleagues.
One of my favourite books Peacock in the Land of Penguins describes the impact attracting different characteristics to an environment, only to try and force them to be something they are not. No spoilers but I bet you can guess the ending.

Why is fit such an important part of culture?

Research by a group of academics on the impact of workers not feeling the fitted in an organisation because of difference, found that many left the organisations where the felt they didn't fit. (5) Sadly, in many cases small adjustments and discussions about concerns the workers were feeling could have resolved negative impact and retained them. Asking workers to change themselves to fit in around the organisation, is not a feasible option.

Case Study - Nicky's story

I have been a PA for around 30 years, a role that involves working under pressure and juggling lots of balls. The worst part for me was feeling that I was losing my cognitive function. At the start of the pandemic, I started a new job. I started to feel that I was absorbing information slower than normal, and I felt under pressure and stressed. After experiencing heart palpitations, I went to my GP who signed me off work for a month. Rather than recognising the need for me to have stability and some adjustments to help me through the worst, I felt that I was being micro-managed, and this added to my stress. I felt I didn't fit any more. When I went back to work, I watched an online menopause talk. It was a lightbulb moment. I realised that I was menopausal. Websites I looked at all focused on hot flushes so I didn't realise that all the symptoms I was getting could be menopause. I had looked at them all in isolation and watching the online talk helped me to link the symptoms together. Suddenly everything made sense.

I'm now in a role that I know really well, and I've had support in understanding my symptoms at work from Occupational Health. However, while it's great having occupational health advice and menopause policies but they are only of value when managers and employees are educated about menopause. Otherwise, nothing changes.

Menopause transition and life stage changes many women's identity so feeling included in an organisation's culture and fitting in, is a balance is a balancing act and potentially very stressful. It's no wonder many women leave the workforce at this stage in their lives.
What should employers do? Research carried out by the CIPD (3) on creating an inclusive culture identifies three features that lead to successful inclusion:

1. Recognition of difference and allowing people to be themselves.
2. Understanding the obstacles to people's development.
3. Trust between groups that allows collaboration.

Organisations can and should talk about menopause and respect and accept the changes that many women will undergo during the transition. Often, they are temporary and can be managed without too much disruption. By understanding menopause, the symptoms and the impact, organisations can work with women to enable them to continue to have a flourishing career. Menopause doesn't have to be the end - I'm going to say it again because I love it so much - Grandmother Hypothesis. Conversation and openness lead to understanding, understanding leads to acceptance, and acceptance leads to inclusion. A culture that celebrates and facilitates inclusion retains talented and valuable menopausal women.

Actions for employers

- Understand your culture - what it's really like to work in your organisation
- Understand how that culture is for menopausal women
- Consider any changes that need to be made to the culture to include menopausal women

- Take steps to make menopause visible and understood so that it becomes a normal feature of your organisation
- Role model respect for mid-life women and women in menopause transition

Epilogue

I'm around ten years into my menopause journey and I can't say that much of it has been a blast. In fact, a lot of it has been pretty rubbish. In lots of ways this makes me sad because I feel like I've lost a chunk of time where I didn't need to feel like I did. With the right treatment and the right workplace conditions I may have had a very different experience. That's why I've written this book. I want other women to know that there is treatment available that can alleviate your symptoms and make your lives better. You must fight for it and be persistent until you get the treatment you need and deserve.

I want employers to know that you have a very important group of employees with experience, knowledge and skills that will be very difficult to replace if they walk out of your doors to retirement, or to an employer who has put in place all of the support that you were thinking about but didn't get round to.

I feel like I am coming out on the other side of my menopause transition, and the fact that I've just written a book while working and with three kids at home makes me think I'm probably doing ok. I've got my brain back. We still have so much to do. Menopause is much more visible and the movement for change has a louder voice, but there are barriers that shouldn't be there. By buying and reading this book, you have donated money to a programme that supports women who otherwise might not have access to treatment and options. This could be for all kinds of reasons, including social deprivation or cancer.

On behalf of those women, thank you for your contribution. You have educated yourself and others on menopause in the workplace and that is a journey that we should all continue.

The work continues and if you would like to know more about how you can help to vital charities in increasing social and economic inclusion, and making menopause better, here are the links:

- Menopause Mandate
  https://www.menopausemandate.com/

- Derby County Community Trust
  https://www.derbycountycommunitytrust.com/

Thank you for your support. May your sleep be unbroken, the names of your colleagues be on the tip of your tongue, and the air conditioning be always functioning.

Resources

Menopause Risk Assessment Template

Date of Assessment:

Function/Department:

Assessor:

Date of next review:

Guidance notes.

Use the list of potential hazards below to identify potential hazards that may affect menopausal women in the workplace. You should tailor the assessment to the type of environment you are assessing. For example, an assessment for someone working in an office environment would have different hazards to a healthcare setting or manufacturing.

When you have identified the risks, add them to the table at the end of this template which will then act as a to do list for the actions and provide a record. Risk assessments should be dynamic and should be reviewed as the circumstances change, or once a year.

1. Concentration/Memory

Potential hazards may include:

Not having sufficient time to do work and still take breaks

Not having access to equipment to make notes

Lack of quiet space to work

2. Tiredness

Potential hazards may include:

Ability to work flexibly

Insufficient breaks

Lack of rest space

Driving and operating equipment

Managing hazardous substances

3. Depression and anxiety

Potential hazards may include:

Excessive workload

No say over the way in which work is carried out

Lack of support in developing skills needed to do the job

Lack of work life balance

Access to mental health support such as counselling

4. Temperature

Potential hazards may include:

Fabric of uniform

Room temperature

Ventilation

Wearing PPE

5. Joints, muscular aches, dizziness

Potential hazards may include:

Workstation

Sitting/standing for long periods of time

Heavy lifting

Insufficient breaks

6. Irregular or heavy periods

Potential hazards may include:

Lack of access to toilets

Access to period products

Access to washing facilities

Risk assessment log

What are the hazards?

Who might be harmed and how?

What are you already doing to control the risks?

What further action do you need to take to control the risks?

Who needs to carry out the action?

When is the action needed by?

(HSE Risk Assessment Template)

References

Chapter 2

What is menopause and how is it impacting the workplace?

1. Caitlin Powell (17 Jan 2022) *One million women could quit due to lack of menopause support, research warns.* People Management. Online. Available at: https://www.peoplemanagement.co.uk/article/1743121/one-million-women-could-quit-due-lack-menopause-support

Chapter 5

Understanding symptoms in a work context

1. Z.Z. Kirshner, Jeffrey K. Yao1, Junyi Li, Tao Long, Doug Nelson, R.B. Gibbs (2020) *Impact of estrogen receptor agonists and model of menopause on enzymes involved in brain*

metabolism, acetyl-CoA production and cholinergic function. Life Sciences 256.

2. Alice Smellie, 7 May 2022. *Testosterone: could it be midlife women's saviour? Experts say the hormone can help with brain function so why isn't it more widely prescribed, asks Alice Smellie.* The Times.

Chapter 6
Knowing menopause rights and responsibilities

1. Guilia Carbonaro (4 August 2022) *Menopause Leave: Is it time for new legal rights to break the stigma in the workplace?* Euronews Next. Online. Available at: https://www.euronews.com/next/2022/08/04/menopause-leave-is-it-time-to-break-stigma-around-menopause-in-the-workplace

2. House of Commons Women and Equalities Committee (28 July 2022) *Menopause and the*

Workplace. HC 91. Online. Available at: https://committees.parliament.uk/work/1416/menopause-and-the-workplace/publications/

3. Yoana Cholteeva (1 June 2022) *Employment Tribunals citing menopause up in 2021, report shows*. People Management. Online. Available at: https://www.peoplemanagement.co.uk/article/1788405/employment-tribunals-citing-menopause-2021-report-shows#:~:text=The%20number%20of%20tribunals%20that,seen%20in%20the%20previous%20year.

4. ACAS Menopause and the law. Online. Available at:https://www.acas.org.uk/menopause-at-work/menopause-and-the-law

5. CIPD (August 2022) *Menopause at Work. A guide for people professionals*. Online. Available at:

https://www.cipd.co.uk/knowledge/culture/well-being/menopause/people-manager-guidance

Chapter 7

Education, education, education

1. CIPD (August 2022) *Menopause at Work. A guide for people managers.* Online. Available at: https://www.cipd.co.uk/Images/line-manager-guide-to-menopause_tcm18-95174.pdf

Chapter 8

Performance management

1. Atkinson C, Beck V, Brewis J, Davies A, Duberley J. (2019) *Menopause and the workplace: New directions in HRM research and HR practice.* Human Resource Management Journal. 2021; 31: 49-64. Online. Available at: https://doi.org/10. 1111/1748-8583.12294

2. CIPD (August 2022) *Performance management: an introduction*. Factsheet, online. Available at: https://www.cipd.co.uk/knowledge/fundamentals/people/performance/factsheet#gref

Chapter 9

Opportunity and promotion in menopause

1. Standard Chartered and Financial Services Skills Commission (October 2021) *Menopause in the Workplace: Impact on Women in Financial Services*. Online. Available at: https://av.sc.com/corp-en/content/docs/Menopause-in-the-Workplace-Impact-on-Women-in-Financial-Services.pdf

2. Beck, V. Brewis, J. Davies, A. (2021) *Women's experiences of menopause at work and performance management.* Organization, 28 (3) pp. 510-520. Online. Available at: http://dx.doi.org/doi:10.1177/1350508419883386

3. Atkinson, C. Ford, J. Harding, N. Jones, F. (2015) The expectations and aspirations of a late-career professional woman. Work, employment and society. 29 (6) pp. 1019-1028. Online. Available at: https://journals.sagepub.com/doi/pdf/10.1177/0950017015581987

4. Burke, V. Grandey, A.A. (2020) *"Midlife Crisis" on the road to successful aging.* Industrial and Organizational Psychology. Bowling Green, 13 (3) pp 388-394. Online. Available at: DOI:10.107/iop2020.62

5. Allison, M. Gale, L. (2021) *New York Times best-selling authors Ms Marcella Allison and Ms Laura Gale present a new mentoring model to help close the gender gap in the C-suite.* Chief of Staff Magazine. Online. Available at: https://www.csa.org/journal/mentoring-model/

Chapter 10

A culture where menopausal women can thrive

1. Edgell, S. and Granter, E. (2020) The Sociology of Work. Continuity and change in paid and unpaid work. London, Sage.

2. Buchanan, D. Huczynski,

3. Jake Young (2019) Creating and developing positive organisational cultures for learning and inclusion. Online. Available at: https://www.cipd.co.uk/news-views/changing-work-views/future-work/thought-pieces/positive-organisational-culture-inclusion

4. BJ Gallacher (2015) Peacock in the Land of Penguins. Oakland, CA. Berrett Kohler.

5. Follmer, E. H., Talbot, D. L., Kristof-Brown, A. L., Astrove, S. L. & Billsberry, J. (2018). Misfits: What do you do when you

can't be yourself at work? LSE Business Review. Online. Available at: https://blogs.lse.ac.uk/businessreview/2018/07/09/misfit-what-do-you-do-when-you-cant-be-yourself-at-work/

Acknowledgements

Where to start with the thank yous? Helping me to create some output started in the most amazing location in Portugal. Jacq Burns and Laura Gale your advice and guidance helped me to take the first step and keep going. My Olhão writing buddies Marcella Allison, Rachel Mazza, John Williams, Anita Chaudhuri, Elizabeth and Mike and Nancy for fun, thoughts and friendship.

Sian Duncan thanks for advice, edits and wine and many HR musings with Karen and Becky. My menopause buddies who keep me going through the brain fog and ranty mood swings, Susie Gahan, Sarah Norton, Tamsin Cook, Mireille Orsini, Helen Perridge and Shirley Roberts.

My fellow menopause warriors Aly Dilks and Laura Biggs and everyone who lends their voice and time to Menopause Mandate, you are an inspirational bunch. Drs Peter Conboy and Paul McNally who gave me my brain and my life back.

This year I have been in awe of the incredible group of people who make up Derby County Community Trust. Your commitment and dedication to social inclusion, equality and opportunity is humbling. I'm so proud to work alongside you all and so grateful to have the opportunity to help. Here's to you and your awesome menopause programme Sharon Dale, Denise Crouch, Hannah Stannier, Lisa Anderson and the support crew Simon Carnall, Paul Newman, Pete Collins and Megan Patrick.

Thank you to my amazing family who have put up with my menopause, and then me writing about my menopause (there is an end to it. Menopause that is, not writing. You just have to be patient. And tolerant.) My mini-mes, Anna, Julia, Robin and Sophie, my lovely Dad and Julie - I'm back in the room. Last but by no means least, editor, best friend, comedian, and so much more, but most of all, love of my life Big Al.

Printed in Great Britain
by Amazon